GETTING TO KNOW THE WORLD'S GREATEST ARTISTS

WINSLOW
HOMER

WRITTEN AND ILLUSTRATED BY MIKE VENEZIA

CHILDREN'S PRESS®
A DIVISION OF SCHOLASTIC INC.
NEW YORK TORONTO LONDON AUCKLAND SYDNEY
MEXICO CITY NEW DELHI HONG KONG
DANBURY, CONNECTICUT

For Mike and Liz, my creative children. Keep up the good work!

Cover: *The Gulf Stream,* by Winslow Homer. 1899, oil on canvas, 28 1/8 x 49 1/8 in.
© Metropolitan Museum of Art, Catharine Lorillard Wolfe Collection, Wolfe Fund, 1906. (06.1234).

Colorist for illustrations: Dave Ludwig

Library of Congress Cataloging-in-Publication Data

Venezia, Mike.
   Winslow Homer / written and illustrated by Mike Venezia.
      p. cm. — (Getting to know the world's greatest artists)
   Summary: A brief biography of the 19th century American artist Winslow
Homer.
   ISBN 0-516-22579-0 (lib. bdg.)   0-516-26979-8 (pbk.)
   1. Homer, Winslow, 1836-1910—Juvenile literature. 2.
Painters—United States—Biography—Juvenile literature. [1. Homer,
Winslow, 1836-1910. 2. Artists.] I. Homer, Winslow, 1836-1910. II.
Title. III. Series.
   ND237.H7V46 2003
   759.13—dc21
                                                2003004591

CHILDREN'S PRESS and associated logos are trademarks
and or registered trademarks of Scholastic Library Publishing.
SCHOLASTIC and associated logos are trademarks and or
registered trademarks of Scholastic Inc.

1 2 3 4 5 6 7 8 9 10 R 13 12 11 10 09 08 07 06 05 04

Winslow Homer with *"The Gulf Stream"* in his painting room at Prout's Neck, by unknown artist.
ca. 1900, albumen print. © Bowdoin College Museum of Art, Brunswick, Maine, Gift of the Homer Family.

Winslow Homer was born in Boston, Massachusetts, in 1836. Winslow always tried to make his watercolors and oil paintings look as realistic and natural as possible. Many people think he is one of the greatest American artists ever.

Long Branch, New Jersey, by Winslow Homer. 1869, oil on canvas, 16 x 21 3/4 in.
© Museum of Fine Arts, Boston, The Hayden Collection-Charles Henry Hayden Fund, 41.631.

Winslow Homer had all kinds of favorite subjects. He often showed people enjoying themselves on vacation. He liked to paint Civil War scenes, and was also interested in picturing the lives of newly freed slaves after the Civil War.

Rainy Day in Camp, by Winslow Homer. 1871, oil on canvas, 20 x 36 in.
© Metropolitan Museum of Art, Gift of Mrs. William F. Milton, 1923. (23.77.1).

Dressing for the Carnival,
by Winslow Homer. 1877,
oil on canvas, 20 x 30 in.
© Metropolitan Museum
of Art, Amelia B. Lazarus
Fund, 1922. (22.220).

Many of Winslow Homer's best works show outdoorsmen in the crisp, clean wilderness areas of northern New England and Canada. Winslow loved being outdoors. He especially liked fishing, hunting, and painting with his older brother, Charles.

Above all, Winslow Homer loved to show the power and danger of the sea.

The Gulf Stream, by Winslow Homer. 1899, oil on canvas, 28 1/8 x 49 1/8 in.
© Metropolitan Museum of Art, Catharine Lorillard Wolfe Collection,
Wolfe Fund, 1906. (06.1234).

The Life Line, by Winslow Homer. 1884, oil on canvas, 28 5/8 x 44 3/4 in.
© Philadelphia Museum of Art, The George W. Elkins Collection, 1924-4-15.

Winslow Homer's family lived pretty close to the sea. His father owned a company that bought and sold goods that arrived on ships from far across the ocean.

Winslow was always interested in drawing while he was growing up. His mother was a talented artist who did watercolors of flowers and plants.

Adolescence, by Winslow Homer. 1846, graphite on paper, 3 9/16 x 4 5/8 in.
© Bowdoin College Museum of Art, Brunswick, Maine, Gift of the Homer Family, 1964.069.008.

Farm Scene, by Winslow Homer. 1847, watercolor and black ink on cardstock, 3 9/16 x 4 15/16 in.
© Bowdoin College Museum of Art, Brunswick, Maine, Gift of the Homer Family, 1964.069.173.

Both of Winslow's parents encouraged their son to draw. Although he got some advice from his mother, Winslow pretty much learned to be an artist all by himself. Winslow did the drawings to the left and above when he was only ten years old.

The Country School, by Winslow Homer. 1871, oil on canvas, 21 1/4 x 38 1/4 in.
© Saint Louis Art Museum, Museum Purchase, 123:1946.

Winslow must have enjoyed grade school.
After he grew up, he painted some scenes
that make school seem pleasant and fun.

Winslow didn't have any desire to go to college, though. He wanted to start making money and living on his own. Fortunately for Winslow, his father had a friend who owned a big printing company in Boston. The owner agreed to give Winslow a job.

Snap the Whip, by Winslow Homer. 1872, oil on canvas, 12 x 20 in.
© Metropolitan Museum of Art, Gift of Christian A. Zabriskie, 1950 (50.41).

Winslow promised
to spend two years
at the printing
company as an
apprentice. He learned
how to make prints,
and spent time practicing his drawing.
Winslow made illustrations for the covers of
sheet music and other printed pieces. Winslow
hated his job, though. He thought the work
was boring and that his bosses were treating
him like a slave.

As soon as the two years were over, Winslow Homer surprised his bosses by leaving his job right away. He felt that he had become a good enough artist to get illustration jobs on his own. Winslow promised himself that he would never work for another boss again—and he never did.

Corner of Winter, Washington and Summer Streets, Boston, by Charles F. Damoreau after Winslow Homer. published 1857, wood engraving on newsprint, 6 5/16 x 9 7/16 in. © National Gallery of Art, Washington, D.C., Avalon Fund, Board of Trustees, 1986.31.137./ PR.

Winslow started to do illustrations for a Boston magazine called *Ballou's Pictorial.* After a short time there, he decided to move to New York City, where there were a lot more magazines that needed illustrations. The editor of the largest magazine in New York, *Harper's Weekly,* liked Winslow's drawings a lot.

The Bathe at Newport, by Winslow Homer. Illustration from Harper's Weekly. © HarpWeek, LLC.

Winslow was offered assignments to draw all kinds of illustrations for *Harper's.* He mainly drew people doing everyday activities in and around the city. The readers of *Harper's Weekly* really enjoyed Winslow's illustrations. Before long, he had become one of the most popular illustrators in the United States.

Thanksgiving in Camp, by Winslow Homer. From Harper's Weekly, November 29, 1862, wood engraving, 9 1/8 x 13 3/4 in. © Metropolitan Museum of Art, Harris Brisbane Dick Fund, 1929. [29.88.3(6)].

In 1861, when the Civil War began, Winslow was asked to travel to battle locations and illustrate what he saw there. Although he drew some battle scenes, he preferred to show the everyday lives of soldiers in camp.

Winslow's most famous Civil War scene, *Prisoners from the Front*, was one of his first oil paintings. It doesn't show any heroic or bloody fighting. Instead it points out the sadness of war in a quiet, thoughtful way.

Prisoners from the Front, by Winslow Homer. 1866, oil on canvas, 24 x 38 in.
© Metropolitan Museum of Art, Gift of Mrs. Frank B. Porter, 1922. (22.207).

Breezing Up (A Fair Wind), by Winslow Homer. 1873-1876, oil on canvas, 24 3/16 x 38 3/16 in. © National Gallery of Art, Washington DC, Gift of the W.L. and May T. Mellon Foundation, Board of Trustees, 1943.13.1.(760)/PA.

Winslow had become interested in oil painting after he moved to New York City. New York had lots of galleries where he could see paintings by other artists. Winslow liked the idea of showing his paintings in a gallery or museum someday.

The Boat Builders, by Winslow Homer. 1873, oil on panel, 6 x 10 1/4 in.
© Indianapolis Museum of Art, Martha Delzell Memorial Fund, IMA54.10.

Winslow continued making illustrations, but started doing more paintings, too. Most of these were about people who lived near the seaside in New Jersey or Massachusetts.

Hermia and Helena, by Washington Allston. Before 1818, oil on canvas, 30 3/8 x 25 1/4 in.
© Art Resource, NY/Smithsonian American Art Museum, Washington, D.C.

Many art critics had problems with Winslow's new paintings. They thought his work didn't fit in with the style of the day. Wealthy people who bought artwork in the 1800s were used to the type of art that had been done in Europe for hundreds of years.

Helen Brought to Paris, by Benjamin West. 1776, oil on canvas, 56 1/2 x 75 3/8 in.
© Art Resource, NY/ Smithsonian American Art Museum, Washington, D.C.

Caius Marius Amidst the Ruins of Carthage,
by John Vanderlyn. 1807, oil on canvas, 87 x 68 1/2 in.
© Fine Arts Museum of San Francisco, Gift of M.H.
de Young, 49835.

Many American artists of the time wanted to please wealthy art buyers. They tried to paint the same way old master artists from France, Holland, and Italy had done. Many of their paintings looked stiff and boring. Also, their paintings had nothing to do with the way most people lived in the United States at the time.

The Gale, by Winslow Homer. 1883-1893, oil on canvas, 30 1/2 x 48 1/2 in.
© Bridgeman Art Library International Ltd., London/New York/Worcester Art Museum, Worcester, Massachusetts.

Most ordinary people didn't agree with the art critics. They liked Winslow's paintings a lot. Since Winslow didn't care what critics thought, he continued to picture people, nature, and natural lighting as they really appeared.

The Blue Boat, by Winslow Homer. 1892, watercolor over graphite pencil on paper, 15 3/16 x 21 1/2 in.
© Museum of Fine Arts, Boston, William Sturgis Bigelow Collection, 26.764.

Winslow never had any interest in showing mythological scenes or showing wealthy people posing in their fanciest clothes.

High Cliff, Coast of Maine, by Winslow Homer. 1894, oil on canvas, 30 1/4 x 38 1/4 in.
© Art Resource, NY/Smithsonian American Art Museum, Washington, D.C.

By sticking to his beliefs about art, Winslow Homer began to create some of the most remarkably realistic paintings ever. Sometimes you can almost feel ocean spray while viewing Winslow's stormy paintings!

Not only did Winslow Homer create a beautiful new style of all-American oil painting, he also helped make watercolor paintings popular. Before he started doing watercolors, artists used them mainly for sketches or to color drawings. Winslow liked watercolors because they were easy to carry around. Also, he could work quickly with them to capture crashing waves, changing light, and shadows.

Winslow learned how to make his paintings shimmer with brightness by letting the white of his paper show through the watery colors.

Under the Coco Palm, by Winslow Homer. 1898, watercolor over graphite on white paper, 38 x 53.8 cm.
© Fogg Art Museum, Harvard University Art Museums, Louise E. Bettens Fund, 2003 President and Fellows of Harvard College.

Except for a few trips to warm, tropical areas, Winslow Homer spent most of his time by the sea in Prout's Neck, Maine. He had a studio there on a rocky cliff above the ocean. Winslow preferred to spend his time alone. He wasn't unfriendly—he just didn't want people interrupting his work.

He sometimes put up signs to scare away amateur artists who came to ask him advice. Winslow concentrated incredibly hard to get the look he wanted. In order to finish the painting below, he waited years for just the right light to come along!

Summer Squall, by Winslow Homer. 1904, oil on canvas, 24 1/4 x 30 1/4 in.
© Sterling and Francine Clark Art Institute, Williamstown, MA.

Winslow Homer died in 1910 at the age of seventy-four. Near the end of his life, he painted fewer paintings with people in them. He concentrated more on the magnificent, stormy ocean crashing against unmovable, rocky cliffs. Winslow seemed to be happiest alone with his favorite subject, the sea.

Works of art in this book can be seen at the following places:

Bowdoin College Museum of Art, Brunswick, ME

Fine Arts Museum of San Francisco

Fogg Art Museum, Cambridge, MA

Indianapolis Museum of Art

Metropolitan Museum of Art, New York

Museum of Fine Arts, Boston

National Gallery of Art, Washington, D.C.

Philadelphia Museum of Art

Saint Louis Art Museum

Smithsonian American Art Museum

Sterling and Francine Clark Art Institute, Williamstown, MA